PLEASE GIVE ME
AN AMAZON REVIEW.
THANK YOU!

D1603811

BERT'S SECRET

THE TRUE STORY OF THE MANHATTAN MADAM

W.R. Wilkerson III

Ciro's
BOOKS

ISBN 978-1-934499-01-6

All family images from the Wilkerson Archives.

Cover design by kafiahmad
Interior design by Amie McCracken

For Don Richardson, who told me this story…

TABLE OF CONTENTS

FROM 1946 TO 1958, Bertha Moskowitz was the most powerful woman in Manhattan. Decades before The Mayflower Madam, or the Hollywood Madam, she came to be known as the Manhattan Madam. She and her girls serviced a veritable Who's Who of New York, from celebrities like the Rat Pack, Bing Crosby and Ed Sullivan, to America's top industrialists, politicians and even the dark world of organized crime. She muled her illegal millions into numbered Swiss bank accounts, and she detested being called grandma. We had to call her Bert...

1

A COOL MEDITERRANEAN breeze wafted in from the ocean, catching Bert's bleach blonde hair and ruffling it momentarily as she and I sat on the balcony enjoying the panoramic view of the harbor below and a room service dinner on that summer evening in 1966. Our family suite at the Hôtel de Paris, the Belle Époque wedding cake hotel of Monaco, perched on the high cliffs above the Mediterranean Sea and nestled beside the famous casino, included a generous balcony that overlooked the ships docked at Port Hercules. But while Bert loved to sit and gaze out at the harbor and the sea, despite its majestic opulence, I hated spending time in Monte Carlo. It was filled with retired white-haired millionaires keeping company with young, beautiful women, who, we all knew, were well paid by their elderly male companions. As a teenager, I felt uncomfortable around these people and couldn't wait to leave the hotel and join up with the friends I'd made on the beach. Yet even finding companions my own age was a challenge. They existed, of course, but as children of the rich and famous, we all shared the same isolation in common that wealth and power provided.

Throughout the 1960s when we vacationed in Monaco, the Hôtel de Paris was our address. These were my family's prosperous halcyon days when we published *The Hollywood Reporter*, the powerful entertainment tabloid Hollywood genuflected in front of. And so Monaco was not a vacation destination for us, it was a place to be noticed.

Throughout my childhood, Bert traveled with us most of the time. Her nights were spent at the historic casino. She would return to our hotel suite in the wee hours, her handbag bursting with French Franc banknotes. Even at a tender age I knew then that when it came to Lady Luck, Bert certainly had the Midas Touch. What I didn't know at the time was that our Monte Carlo sojourns, apart from seeking attention from high society, were, in fact, whistle-stops to acquire financing.

Years later I would learn that Bert's successful gambling sprees not only paid for our luxurious French Riviera visits but also for the rest of our European excursions.

Her name was Alberta Miles, and she was my grand- mother by marriage. She insisted on being

Bert with valise filled with gambling wins by her side. Monte Carlo, 1967.

called Bert because she hated being called gram or grandma. The petite blonde with periwinkle eyes and perfectly coiffed hair would sit across from me donning coquettish dresses and more makeup than I had ever seen on any woman.

Between sips of wine and delicate tiny mouthfuls of sole dipped in lemon butter on that balcony, she loved asking questions—about me, my interests—and then offering grandmotherly advice. Bert was the one person in my family who listened and paid attention to me, who encouraged and stood by me, although this loyalty would be challenged a few years later. She became one of the most influential figures of my teenage years. And in this way Bert lit up the time in Monaco, that is, until one particular evening in 1966, when she asked me a question that irrevocably changed the nature of our relationship, and, unbeknownst to me until many years later, offered me a glimpse into the true landscape of her wild and scandalous past.

The summer dusk sky dissolved into a pastel pink hue highlighting Bert's face as she gazed out at the bobbing boats on the waterline and the light flickering across the green sea below us. I, on the other hand, had the manners and appetite of a thirteen-year-old boy and my behavior reflected it—I was devouring my beef stroganoff.

"How's the stroganoff?" Bert asked. The question was irrelevant.

I nodded in exuberance and gastronomical ecstasy. I knew better than to speak with my mouth full in front of Bert.

She observed me chewing and swallowing and then hit me with the question that changed everything.

"Do you carry condoms?"

Had she pulled out a .357 magnum and shot me it wouldn't have been any different.

I choked. Bert waited for me to stop coughing.

"You should." She delicately touched the corner of her mouth with her cloth napkin. "You should always be prepared. How old are you now?"

"Almost fourteen," I said. "Fourteen in October."

"You're old enough. Have you had sex yet?"

Bert on the family yacht.
Cannes, France, 1966.

"No!" I said emphatically.

Thinking this was some kind of setup, I was cautious about what I said next. The casual, friendly mood I normally enjoyed with Bert dissolved in an instant.

"Well," said Bert, raising her coffee cup with a dainty hand and taking a sip. "It's time to be prepared. And careful of the partners you choose."

The meat on my plate, which, a moment earlier I had been vacuuming with such gusto, suddenly no longer looked appetizing. I raised my eyes slowly to meet Bert's. She looked the same to me and yet completely different at the same time. Then came her all-knowing Mona Lisa smile, signaling a secret had been passed between us and it was safe with her.

None of my relatives talked about sex, so Bert's lecture was the seminal incident that would eventually help me decode her entire life. I have no memory of how we spent the rest of that evening together or even the days that followed. I still loved Bert and still experienced her as my most steadfast champion among my emotionally chaotic family. But after that brief exchange, I was less open with her. I began to feel almost naked around her, as if she could see through

Even in illness, Bert's sense of humor was still intact. Bel-Air, 1969.

me—the young boy careening headlong into adolescence and young adulthood.

In fact, I think I was right.

I never asked Bert for anything, particularly after her 1966 sex lecture on that French Riviera balcony. But there was one time I needed her help, and I was reluctant to ask for it. Yet she was the only person I felt I could turn to.

In December 1969, I was home from boarding school in England. I got a Christmas job at the William Morris Agency in Beverly Hills as a runner so that I could save up enough money to buy my own guitar. Every free moment I had at school, I played music. I had grown weary of borrowing guitars from other students. In conjunction

Bert in Bel-Air, 1966.

with a school savings account at Bank of America I had had since I was seven years old, and what I earned at William Morris, I had enough money to buy a Martin D-28 acoustic guitar. I purchased it from a black market vendor in downtown LA for $250 and quickly spirited it under my bed because of the disapproval I knew it would generate from my parents. The plan was to get it back to England, and that plan involved Bert.

At the time, Bert was living with us in Bel-Air. I would like to say that she was in wonderful health but in fact she was bedridden with terminal cancer, which was the reason she was staying with us in the first place. Every day when I got home from my job at William Morris, I would sit by her bed and talk to her, holding her wan hand in mine. A few minutes into one visit with Bert, I announced that I had purchased a guitar.

"That's wonderful," Bert said. "Is it the one you wanted?"

I nodded. "But I need a favor. Can you say the guitar is from you, like a Christmas present?"

"Do you want the money for it?"

"No," I said. "Just say it was from you when they ask."

She winked. "No problem."

"They" referred to her son Bill Miles, my mother's husband, and my mother.

I was forbidden to own a guitar. My grades at school were poor, and both my mother and Bill thought the instrument would only pose an additional and unnecessary distraction that would compound my poor school performance. I, of course, saw it differently. Playing music was my life. It brought me an unparalleled joy that surpassed everything else. To me, this happiness could only translate into my potential academic success.

Bill conducted frequent raids through my room, mainly looking for drugs and other items he deemed contraband. He often confiscated many personal items he believed did not belong to me. So, I suppose it was inevitable he would find the guitar under my bed. It was the day after Christmas. He convened a family meeting in our living room which had all the trappings of a court-martial. Present were my mother, Bert, my sister Cindy, my stepsister Laura, my stepbrother Jeffrey, and, of course, Bill, who acted as interrogator, prosecutor, and executioner.

As the black guitar case stood in the middle of the living room as Exhibit A, Bill thundered to everyone present that I had purchased the guitar without consulting them. Everyone in the room knew that music was my siren song and that the only thing in the world I wanted was a guitar. And so I had to sit there for twenty-five minutes while Bill painted me a deceitful, despicable teenager in every color of the rainbow.

I waited for Bert to chime in. She never did.

I never trusted her after that.

When Bill finished his tirade, he whisked the guitar away and, after that, I never went to go see Bert in her room. She had made me a promise and had broken it.

But five days later, on New Year's Eve, much to my surprise, Bill demanded that I follow him. We walked out to the garage where he opened the trunk of his silver Bentley. There was my guitar lying in peaceful repose.

"Take it," he barked.

I didn't ask why. Stunned, I plucked the guitar from the trunk and before I had a chance to thank him, he slammed the trunk lid shut and stormed off in a huff.

A week after getting my guitar back, I strapped it carefully into the back seat of a yellow cab. After making sure it was secure, I made one final trip inside the house to say goodbye to Bert. She winked at me. "You got your guitar," she said. It was then I knew she had something to do with its return. A bolt of pure joy radiated throughout my entire body.

I kissed her on the forehead. It was the last time I saw her.

I climbed into the cab that transported me to the airport and back to England. The cancer she fought so bravely against finally claimed her in July 1970. She was seventy-two. Upon learning the news in England, I wept for days.

But it was in 1992 I would come to learn that this woman I had loved so much had led a double life.

2

THE FACTS came to me from an unlikely source. British biographer Robert Lacey was in Los Angeles researching a book on screen goddess Grace Kelly in 1992. We had planned to dine together, but he apologetically canceled at the last moment. Someone he desperately needed to speak to for his book had called and agreed to an interview that evening.

The following morning, Robert phoned to tell me that the subject of his interview the previous evening turned out to be none other than my uncle-in-law, Don Richardson. Don, he said, was very anxious to talk to me. Don had been married to Bert's daughter, Reneé, in the mid-1950s. I hadn't seen him since Bert's passing in 1970. But when I called him that night, he made it clear he needed to see me right away. The urgency in his voice was undeniable.

I liked Don. He, like Bert, was one of the few people in my family who also paid attention to me. We were both artists and so we always had things in common to talk about.

Late the following afternoon I arrived at Don's beige bungalow house in Van Nuys, California. It was simple and understated—hardly the palace one would come to associate with one of Hollywood's leading TV directors of the 1950s and '60s. Don, sporting a full beard, greeted me with an enthusiastic bear hug on the doorstep. "Been a long time," he said.

After divorcing Bert's daughter in 1969, Don married a woman decades his junior who, according to him, finally brought him the peace and happiness he had so yearned for in his chaotic and turbulent life.

"Have a seat," he said, pointing to the couch in the living room before disappearing into a small kitchen. I sank into Don's heavily pillowed, white living room sofa. His house was very well kept. Inside the walls were covered with faithful copies he'd painted of famous impressionist paintings. I distinctly remember a copy of a Monet hanging above the mantlepiece. I had always admired Don's skill as a painter.

He returned, a glass of Perrier with ice and lime for me and a glass of red wine for himself, and sat on the couch next to me. At first, Don made small talk, bringing me up-to-date on his life. During my childhood and young adulthood, he had been a busy TV director. At first, I thought he'd aged out of TV work some years back. Instead, he had moved into teaching and was on the faculty at UCLA. From the coffee table, he handed me a copy of his book on method acting.

"Actually," he said, "I didn't age my way out of directing. I drank myself out of it."

Don was always a straight shooter, which was one of things I loved about him.

"But listen," he said, "the real reason I wanted you to come over was to talk about Alberta."

I felt my eyebrows rise. "Bert?"

"I always called her Alberta," he said with affection.

Bert had been gone for more than twenty years. What could he possibly tell me about my grandmother?

"Bert was…not who you think she was."

"What the hell does that mean?" I said.

"What do you know about Alberta?"

I confessed I only knew her as my grandmother and that she was a seminal part of my upbringing. I also added that I missed her.

But just the tone of Don's voice made me uneasy. I stared at the ice cubes melting into my sparkling water. Don, bless him, always an intuitive guy, caught the sense of my discomfort.

"Oh, she was your grandmother, all right. And she adored you. But did you ever wonder where all her money came from?"

Growing up, my siblings and I were told that Bert was independently wealthy. It was the answer we bought as kids. I was so caught up in my own teenage yearnings and disappointments, I never pulled back the lens on my own family to notice how nothing lined up in a normal, orderly way.

"Well, I'm gonna tell you a story that's gonna blow your fuckin' mind," he said. "Ever heard of Polly Adler?"

I shook my head.

"Polly Adler was the most successful madam in this country up until the end of the Second World War. She and her girls serviced mobsters like Dutch Schultz and even New York's Mayor, Jimmy Walker, back in the prohibition days. But you've heard of The Mayflower Madam, right?"

"Who hasn't," I said. Sydney Biddle Barrows, otherwise known as The Mayflower Madam, had featured prominently in the news when her high-end escort business that catered to industrialists, high-powered business executives, lawyers, foreign diplomats, and even Arabian oil sheiks was busted in 1984. Her takedown reverberated from coast to coast.

"Now this is going to come as a shock to you, but Alberta, our Alberta, surpassed Polly Adler's and even the The Mayflower Madam's success. She became the wealthiest and most powerful madam in this country during the late forties and fifties."

"You're telling me Bert was a hooker?"

"No, she was a madam."

I learned later that a madam is typically an ex-prostitute in charge of multiple prostitutes.

Don went on to add that she had spent decades as the proprietor of a prestigious Manhattan prostitution ring.

I sat on his couch in stunned disbelief. I already came from a complicated family. My father, Billy Wilkerson, had been a major power player in Hollywood for decades and had strong mob ties with gangsters like Johnny Rosselli and Bugsy Siegel. He was also the proprietor of a string of Golden Era nightclubs and restaurants which became the stuff of legend—venues like Café Trocadero, Ciro's, Vendome, LaRue, and, in Las Vegas, The Flamingo Hotel.

But now I was being told that this woman I had put up on a pedestal was anything but the woman I knew.

3

BERT WAS BORN Bertha Moskowitz, the only daughter of Louis and Rosie Moskowitz in Iasi, Romania on March 17, 1898. Around 1914, the family escaped Jewish persecution in their homeland and fled to the US where they made a home in New York City. Unfortunately, one of the many secrets Bert took to her grave was her life prior to 1920. On March 21, 1920, she married silent film producer Herbert Leroy Miles in Manhattan, New York and during their marriage, they had two children, William Jr. and Reneé. One day William Jr., or Bill as we knew him, would come to be my imposing and bullying stepfather. But that would happen decades later.

Apparently, William Sr. had an eye for the ladies and contracted syphilis in 1927.

"That did it," said Don. Bert took the kids and moved out. Up until that point, she had been a housewife. She had little formal education according to Don and was not skilled at anything. And so, it didn't take her long to realize that there weren't many employment options for a twenty-nine-year-old woman in her situation.

Don looked me right in the eye now. "Alberta was a smart cookie—and ambitious. It's hard to picture it now but back in the day she was a looker. So, she turned to the oldest profession in the world."[1]

His words worked themselves slowly into the folds of my brain.

Don made it clear that Bert quickly discovered she had a formidable hands-on understanding for seeing right through most heterosexual males, an innate experiential knowledge of what most men wanted.

He began to describe how Bert cunningly built her empire. By the late 1940s she had enough money saved from prostitution to open a nightclub in New York City on 73rd Street and 3rd Avenue. In those days, this part of the Upper East Side wasn't fancy. It was a middle-class neighborhood—full of brownstones and no distinguishing landmarks. This nightclub was called The Executive Suite and from the street looked like just another vacant store with the windows painted solid. No name appeared on the establishment. "You just had to know where to look," Don recalled.

The inside, too, was simple. Almost shockingly modest, it resembled an unfurnished bar or tavern. Don, who was an eyewitness, remembers that it had a little understated bar which, on the countertop, sat a number of black dial-up telephones. But sitting on bent wire chairs at tiny bare tables were, according to Don "some of the most beautiful women in New York City."

Don adamantly stressed that The Executive Suite was not technically a whorehouse because Bert did not do the arranging. Her girls did. At the club, her girls acted as hostesses. Don was clear that Bert just presented them. Bert merely thought of herself as a manager and the madam of the bar, who table-hopped and chatted with all her celebrity clients. She let her girls make their own decisions—who, where and how much to charge. It was an approach that was not only brilliant but revolutionary. By giving her hostesses real authority and autonomy, and a place where they could conduct their business, Bert was way ahead of her time in giving her female talent the decision-making power. I could sense Don's admiration.

Clients would meet up with dates at The Executive Suite and then the girls would take them back to elegant hotels like The Astor, The Plaza, or The Waldorf. Don said the girls had arrangements with all the hotels, who also got their cut. The men never paid Bert directly. "She got her cut from the girls later," Don remembered. "And she made millions—and I mean *millions*."

Decades before The Mayflower Madam, or the Hollywood Madam, Bert was the Manhattan Madam. If Polly Adler was the madam who ran New York's most exclusive brothel in the 1930s, it was Bert who inherited her mantel after Adler retired in 1944. By the late 1940s, Bert and her girls would come to service a Who's Who of the rich and famous, from celebrities to industrialists, to politicians and even high-ranking figures in organized crime. What was becoming clear to me now was that this woman who had assumed this brilliant subterfuge as my own grandmother was one of the most powerful and independently wealthy women of her era. And that, in and of itself, was a rarity.

4

Don Richardson met Bert in 1958. At the time, he was one of TV's most sought-after directors, helming *The United States Steel Hour* in the 1950s, and such iconic 1960s hits as *Bonanza* and *Lost in Space*. He was also responsible for numerous TV specials.

Don was an attractive, successful man, dating Reneé Miles, Bert's redheaded daughter, in 1957. I never asked him how they met, but when the two became engaged, Bert dispatched her son, Bill, to investigate the TV director. The two had a couple of drinks in Don's studio on Waverly Place in Greenwich Village, and Bill reported back to his mother that his sister's fiancé was a reputable television director, making very good money.

"The US Steel Company was paying me upwards of $4,000 ($37,914.79 in 2021) a week," said Don.[2]

All Bert wanted to know was whether Don was making a living. She invited him to her club a few days later. Don sat down at a table with Reneé and noticed right away the pairing up of celebrities with gorgeous girls.

"I just thought it was like a night spot," said Don. "You know, a private little drinking club."

Bert introduced herself, and Don immediately found her adorable. But… "She had a head full of shit like Shirley McLaine," noted Don. "You know, romance and astrology, that kind of thing."

After Don and Reneé married in 1958, Bert and Bill Miles showed no interest at all in the newlyweds, or in Don's increasingly prominent career. Don recounted how one night he and a gigolo friend of Bill's were watching Don Juan in Hell, starring George C. Scott on a television set in Bill Miles' Manhattan apartment as they waited for Bill to finish dressing so they could go out.

"Hey, this is a hell of a show," said the gigolo.

"Yeah," Don agreed. "It is."

The end credits rolled and Don's name came up as the director.

"Hey, isn't that you?" said the gigolo.

"Yeah," said Don.

"Bill never said you do that."

Recalling the moment, Don laughed. "I was like some bum who was lucky to be married to his sister."

As a wedding gift, Bert gave the couple a grand tour of Europe. Oddly, Bill and Bert accompanied them. One night on a sleeper train from Paris to Geneva, Reneé and Don were in the compartment next to Bert and Bill. Don could hear mother and son arguing. He put an ear up to the compartment wall to hear better.

"It was the goddamndest thing to listen to them," Don said. "They were just scheming and talking about the banks in Switzerland and future plans and all of that. They were like collaborating."

Bert's club was a cash business generating millions. Once they hit Geneva, Bert and Bill mysteriously excused themselves. It was then Don learned the real reason why the two had tagged along. "They were muling the club's money into Switzerland," Don said. "They were making deposits into unnamed numbered accounts. Bill carried the money, and Alberta banked it."

Three months later, Bert took the couple to Europe again. After they had checked in for their flight at New York's Idlewild Airport (now JFK), Bill Miles ushered Don into the men's room. After making make sure they were alone, Bill herded the TV director into an empty stall and locked the door behind them. He handed Don a bulging black leather fanny pack.

"Here, put this on," Bill commanded.

"What the hell is it?" said Don.

"It's a money belt."

Don protested. "I don't want to do that, for Christ's sake."

"Aw, come on," Bill said. "We do it all the time."

"Hey, I work for the US Steel Company. I can't get into this."

"Everybody does it," said Bill. "Alberta's taking her profits abroad, that's all."

Don was adamant. "I can't do it."

Bill became impatient. In a tone Don recalled as distinctly menacing, his new brother-in-law said, "How much do you like your career?"

There wasn't a question. "I knew exactly what he meant," said Don.

A single phone call, a hint of any scandal, Don went on to say, could easily and quickly erase his successful career. "And so I, like an idiot, put on the fucking belt."

During the flight Don went into the restroom to examine the belt. When he unzipped it, he felt the blood drain from his face. It was stuffed with a quarter of a million dollars in cash.

"It was then I knew I was cooked," Don confessed. "I'd married into a mafia family."

5

DON RECALLED Bill Miles as being a mysterious Tyrone Power type: handsome, sleek with dark hair neatly combed back, and who spoke several languages. It wasn't long before Don found out Bill had the reputation for breaking hearts and bank accounts. He wasted no time proudly showing off his bedroom to his brother-in-law. "He was particularly proud of the décor," he noted. Bill had cupids painted above the bed. He opened the night table drawer which revealed dildos, a blow-up vagina, a package of French ticklers, and the *Kama Sutra*."

Don couldn't underscore more forcefully how relentless Bill's gigolo lifestyle was. He was privy to it on several occasions. He remembered a wealthy English couple came to stay at Bill's apartment for a few days. Don recalled the wife as a petite, dark-haired Vivian Leigh lookalike. But what really annoyed him, he said, was that her undergarments were hung up all through the apartment, strung up on lines in the living room, the kitchen, and the hallway.

One evening the husband and Don were having drinks in the living room. The wife and Bill disappeared into the bedroom and shut the door. As the two men in the living room rapidly drained an entire fifth of scotch, Don became worried.

"I watched to see if anybody was going to kill anybody," he said. "But the guy [the husband] wasn't doing anything about it."

To distract himself from what was going on in the bedroom, the husband showed Don a Hasselblad camera set which he had paid handsomely for that afternoon.

One night, Bill took Don along to a dinner party across the street. It was the penthouse owned by the chief attorney for a major circus company. Don alleged it was the Barnum & Bailey Circus. He and Bill were both attired in dinner jackets. Bill's platinum and diamond studs were in hock, and so Don had to pin his sleeves up with paper clips.

At the attorney's penthouse apartment, the two men were greeted by a striking French woman, perhaps in her mid-thirties, who kissed Bill on the lips. There was also a pretty young girl of about fifteen who also kissed Bill on the lips. The three of them sat on the couch. The mother nibbled on Bill's neck and put her hand inside his shirt while the daughter sat on his lap, wiggled a lot, and blew in his ear.

While all this was going on, Don chatted with the woman's husband, who was making martinis with Russian vodka. "They were the greatest martinis I ever drank in my life," Don commented.

The husband was a dignified man, in his early sixties, who paid no attention to the trio on the couch.

When Bill and Don returned to their apartment, the TV director couldn't contain himself. "Jesus," he said, "what is that whole arrangement there? Are you fucking the daughter and the mother?"

"Yeah," Bill confessed.

"The kid's only about fifteen. It's statutory rape."

Bill removed the paper clips from his shirt and placed them on his dresser. "They're not going to squeal."

"What's with the man?"

"He's got a bad back. He wears some kind of a corset, brace or something. He can't fuck his wife. So he tolerates our arrangement. As a matter of fact he gives me money."

Don discovered that these "arrangements" were common for Bill Miles. Yet despite being paid well for his services, the Manhattan gigolo was always broke.

"He put the touch on me every time he went out the door," said Don. "He'd say, 'You got a fifty on you? I'll give it back tomorrow.' I never saw a nickel."

Don was anxious to separate his life from his dubious in-laws. He and Renée moved from New York to Hollywood in the late 1950s to be closer to industry work. When Don returned to New York in 1961 to direct *The Defenders*, he was booked in at The Algonquin. When Bert found out, however, she insisted he stay at her son's apartment as he was family now. Bill gave his brother-in-law the back room "where the maid's cleaning shit was kept" and charged him rent.

Don noticed that Bill had a penchant for frequenting society parties. "Who knows, he was probably cruising for clients," said Don. Apparently Bill loved parties where they had raffles, treasure hunts, and other party games. One night he dragged Don out of bed at 1 a.m. and out into the hallway to help him lug a huge crate of beer he had won in a party game.

"Bill was so excited," Don remembered. "And he didn't even drink beer."

Yet this man Don had written off as a mere cad also mysteriously moved in high circles that accorded him the same affection.

One night in Rome, Bill asked Don if he would like to meet Federico Fellini, the iconic Italian film director.

"I always thought he was full of shit," Don said, "but I thought 'who knows?'"

The two drove quite a distance out on the Appian Way in the dead of night to an enormous house with a pool carved into a cliffside. It belonged to film producer, Dino De Laurentiis, and his wife, Silvana Mangano. It seemed as if the entire Italian film industry was in attendance, and Bill was on affectionate terms with all of them. As guests arrived, they hugged and kissed him. When Fellini walked in, Don watched as he and his wife, Messina, the lady in *La Strada*, "who had the worst body odor," kissed and embraced Bill like an old friend.

At first, Don was mystified by Bill Miles' connection to this elite throng. But upon reflection, it was his contention that Bill was funneling some of Bert's enormous fortune into the Italian film industry. "How else would he know these people?" said Don. "He [Bill Miles] wasn't in this business [the film industry], and you don't get to know these people unless there's some kind of business connection. There had to be some kind of funding going on." During his life, De Laurentiis insisted that none of his films were mafia financed. But money coming from Bert was, in fact, mafia money.

6

It was Bill Miles' ultimate ambition to marry a wealthy woman from a prominent family, and in his mind, it was his mother's profession, and not his own, that interfered with his social climbing. He felt it was ruining his life, and he hated her for it.

"If they found out Alberta was a hooker," said Don, "he was out of business with Sacony Oil, the Rockefellers, and the Kennedys."

Bert on the other hand would do anything for her son. She paid his considerable rent. She bought him a filling station, which Bill sold for under value to pay gambling debts. When he went to Europe for two years, he supported himself by forging his mother's name on checks.

"You see how much I love him that I didn't put him in jail?" Bert said to Don when she discovered the check cashing fraud.

When Bert talked about her son, it was beyond elevation.

"She would talk about him as though he was the greatest cocksman that ever lived," Don said. "How lucky the women were who had her son as a lover."

Bert would set him up with her girls without pay.

"She felt she was doing her girls a great favor," Don added.

Don steadfastly maintained that Bert was romantically in love with her own son.[3] He again cited the sleeper train incident when he caught the couples' scheming through the compartment wall as they raced through Europe at night. "I was itching to hear any sounds of kissing or cock-sucking," he said.

Bert promised her son that she would retire. But it came too late. On Thursday, November 6, 1958, Don's phone rang at 2 a.m. It was Bert making her one phone call from jail. Don and Reneé found Bert and two of her girls, still in their minks, behind bars with the other street whores. It was Bill Miles' worst fears come true.[4]

"That's when I found out Alberta was a hooker," said Don.

Bert and two of her $100 girls were seized in a suite at the Warwick Hotel on 54th Street and 6th Avenue and were taken into police custody. At the station, Bert was identified as the manager. The news articles that appeared the following day said that Bert and her girls were soliciting clients at the club. But Don remembers it differently. There was a private party at the hotel for two of the Rockefeller nephews. The cops caught Bert's girls naked in the bedroom while Bert was sitting in the outer room waiting in her mink. Don said the police were careful not to involve the Rockefellers and kept them out of the papers.

Don paid their bails, which amounted to $600 ($5,569.55 in 2021), as Bert wept.

4-Fri., Nov. 7, 1958   ★★★★★ New York Journal American

THE EXECUTIVE SUITE!

Cops Call on 2 Girls—Find More Than Cupboard Bare

Woman Held As 'Manager'

Two alleged $100-a-date call girls and their reported "manager" were arrested early today in a police raid personally led by Deputy Police Commr. James R. Kennedy.

The suspects were two of some half dozen girls reportedly operating out of a 3d ave. tavern which police had under surveillance before the raiders swooped down at 2 a.m.

The women were identified as Maria Martinez, 24, a long-haired brunette, of 404 E. 74th st., and Joan Martin, 25, a good looking blonde, of 415 E. 63d st. Their "manager" was identified as Mrs. Alberta Miles, 42, of 25 E. 83d st., who runs the Executive Suite Tavern, 73d st, and 3d ave.

The alleged call girls were seized in a suite at the Warwick Hotel, 54th st. and 6th ave., when a raiding party opened the door with a pass key. Kennedy said neither girl wore any clothes,

Their two dates were released after questioning but were to be called as witnesses in Women's Court today, Kennedy said.

POLICE IN TAVERN

The Commissioner said three detectives under Lt. Thomas Dorrin entered the tavern shortly after midnight to prepare for the raid. Some time after their entrance, Kennedy said, Mrs. Miles asked two businessmen at a neighboring table: "Would you like some girls?" She then brought the Martin

SEIZED IN RAID . . . Brunette Maria Martinez, 24, of 404 E. 74th st., and blonde Joan Martin (rear), 25, of 415 E. 63d st., alleged call girls, are shown in the W. 54th st. precinct after their arrest early today. Journal-American Photo by Leo Morgan

and Martinez girls over and the dates were made, according to police. The men left the tavern some time before the girls to make arrangements at the War-wick, Kennedy said.

The Commissioner said his office had received complaints about the tavern "from a number of sources."

Bert's police bust. New York, 1958.

43

Upon learning the news from his precinct and anticipating the arrival of newspaper photographers, a lieutenant
had hurried from his home in full dress uniform. He was
still buttoning up his uniform when he rushed up to Bert.
He apologized to her profusely, Don recalls. He kissed her
on both cheeks and hugged her.

"I'm sorry, Alberta," said the contrite lieutenant. "The
guy's a jerk," he said, referring to his new police boss. "This
will never happen again."

Bert's police raid had been initiated by a new deputy
police commander, James R. Kennedy. Don recalled that
every new police commander would arrest hookers to teach
them a lesson. "From then on," he said, "the police were in on
the cut. That's how it was done."

Bert had always made her payoffs religiously to the cops,
judges, and politicians. "Alberta paid for years and years and
years," remarked Don. But in the end, the payoffs couldn't
protect her.

Normally after a high-profile prostitution bust, there
most likely would have been an inquiry into tax evasion of
which Bert would have also been busted for. But Don noted
that Bert had very powerful clients in the IRS who looked
the other way.

"I never found out exactly how it [the bust] was finally
resolved," said Don. For certain, Bert never did any jailtime
for her arrest.

It's common knowledge that madams keep a black book.
"It's the one thing johns live in dread of," Don remarked,
"because in the event of a bust, there's the real possi-
bility the madam will do anything for a lighter sentence."

Anticipating this reality, Bert never kept any kind of a book. Her girls did. The theory was if the girl was busted, it was on her whether to cooperate or not. As sweet and angelic as Bert seemed to Don, her ruthlessness chilled his blood. "In the end she was prepared to hang her girls out to dry to save herself," he remarked.

Don and his wife walked a shaken Bert to the car and drove her home. With the incident breaking in the papers, Bill Miles' dream of marrying a Rockefeller or Kennedy was over.

7

AFTER HER police bust, Bert finally saw the writing on the wall. Her fabulous run of success was over. Almost immediately, she closed The Executive Suite and from then on, she made no secret of her profession to her son-in-law. She came to see in Don an ally and confidant. Yet despite her high-profile arrest, Bert continued to service clients well into her fifties. Don said Bert had a little apartment near Bloomingdales. Once when he picked her up to take her to dinner, she came to the door in her robe. Emerging from the bedroom and stuffing his white shirt into his pants was a large-bellied man. Bert introduced the two men and over dinner she disclosed to Don that he was one of the heads of the US Steel Company.

After The Executive Suite folded, Bert felt free to disclose her former business with her son-in-law. She had painted a very clear picture that as far as exclusivity went, she and her girls had cornered the Manhattan market. It was a small clientele, but A-List. Bert confessed that Bing Crosby would hole up in a New York hotel for a week or two at a time and call her for hookers. He generally stayed drunk, but he liked the girls to be around, naked. Sammy Davis, Jr. apparently was a great favorite of all the hookers.

"They thought he was such a great bang that they practically did it for nothing," Don recalled Bert telling him.

Ed Sullivan, the famous variety show impresario, used to call Bert and ask her to send over a girl. He would have her walk around the apartment naked and just look at her. Frank Sinatra brought a little attaché case with dainty aprons, which he liked to have the girls put on when they were naked. Then he liked pulling the bow in the back.

"She never used a dirty word the whole time I knew her," Don noted. "She always talked about 'clean' girls."

A number of Bert's girls went on to marry their celebrity clients. "The *Pretty Woman* syndrome." Don laughed. He noted that Norma Storch, the wife of comedian Larry Storch, was one of Bert's $50 girls, as was Alicia Buttons, the wife of legendary comedian Red Buttons. Many of these women I knew personally as they dined at our home frequently. But I was clueless to their backstories. That was all part of Bert's secret.

But while Bert freely discussed her celebrity clients with Don, she rarely disclosed who her political clients were and never revealed those in organized crime she had traffic with. "She just never talked about them," said Don. Perhaps those connections were still active or too sensitive. There was, however, one exception. Papa Louie.

"Papa Louie," said Don, "was the final word on whether you lived or died." Louie was a mafia judge who did not work within the judicial system we're familiar with. He presided over trials of his own kind. Apparently even the underworld had their own penal code.

Papa Louie's real identity is lost to us. We know nothing about him, not even his real name. Obviously a nickname, there's no record of any Papa Louie who was active in organized crime in New York during the period Bert was in business. The argument can be made then that Louie wasn't even a gangster at all. But to assume we know all the individuals connected with organized crime over the decades is simply naïve. While the actual percentage is not known to us, it's extremely likely that a considerable portion of figures working in crime rings in America slipped through the cracks of history and successfully evaded law enforcement's radar screen simply because they never wound up on a police blotter. Don firmly believed that this was the case with Papa Louie.

Bert said she met Papa on an ocean liner to Europe. "She was probably working her way over," Don said.

Papa lived in Harlem in what looked like a tenement on the outside. But inside, through the entryway, the entire building had been gutted and transformed. It was redone with elevators, guardrooms, and holding pens for wiseguys who had misbehaved. His own apartment, an enormous duplex on the top floor, was decorated in the style of a Chinese restaurant, complete with plaster Buddhas. "Papa was crazy for anything Chinese," said Don.

Don couldn't tell me how long Bert and Papa dated, but Papa certainly considered Bert his girlfriend. While Bert got considerable mafia backing and protection from her other clients in organized crime, "Dating Papa Louie," Don remarked, "was like dating the Pope of the crime word."

Bert used to arrive with cartons of Chinese take-out, which Papa loved. She went to any extent to indulge him. While he sat in judgment surrounded by his henchmen, deciding the fate of some quivering culprit in front of him, Bert would be under the covered table, exercising her skills.

"She considered that one of the great triumphs of her life." Don laughed.

Bert told her son-in-law that Papa was killed in an intentional car ramming from a rival gang in the mid-1950s.

"She never got over his death," Don remarked.

8

I FIRST MET Bill Miles one summer Southern California day in 1964 when he drove up to our Bel-Air house in a pale blue Lincoln Continental wearing a blue button-down Brooks Brothers shirt and Gucci loafers with no socks. He came to court mom.

As the feminist publisher of *The Hollywood Reporter*, the powerful industry tabloid that brought news and gossip to the entertainment world, my mom, Tichi Wilkerson, was a major Hollywood power player, easily making her one of the most influential women in the industry. She also

New York City gigolo,
Bill Miles, 1967.

commanded enormous respect as a community leader. As the founder of Women in Film, for example, she was responsible for creating the organization that finally empowered women in the entertainment industry to realize their potential. All this made her quite a catch.

Bert and Tichi Wilkerson on their final European trip, 1968.

According to Don, Bert financed her son's entire courtship, forking out close to $20,000 on a Rodeo Drive wardrobe she hand-picked for him and paying cash for the new pale blue Lincoln. Lastly, she stuffed his bank account for entertaining and arranged restaurants for their dates. Bert, who was determined to marry her son off to wealth, felt that they had struck gold with my mom and Bert was going to do everything in her power to make sure this opportunity wasn't blown.

Bill and Tichi courting, 1964.

After a short, whirl-wind courtship, the couple married at a civil judge's home in Palm Springs, California in early 1965. It was a major coup for the New York City gigolo who had given up all hopes of any social standing. But it didn't take long for Tichi's mother, Beatrice Noble, to start asking questions.

Bill Miles, W.R. Wilkerson, and Tichi Wilkerson. Los Angeles, 1965.

Gram was a short, stocky, red-haired Hispanic matron who demanded to know what Bill did for a living. Bill claimed that he was a dealer in Arabian horses, but we never saw any horses. Friends advised Mom to hire a private detective and cautioned her to do some background digging on Bill before getting hitched. She refused. She could see by Bert's lifestyle that she was a woman of considerable means, and when she asked her fiancé how Bert supported herself, Bill said she owned a seat on the New York Stock Exchange and did well with her investments.

"Bill always had a story," Don said.

While Mom was satisfied with the answers, Gram was not. Her demands to see evidence of Bill's occupation became deafening.

In order to take the heat off, Bill and Bert decided that she should take Gram on a trip to Las Vegas. But instead of bottling up the genie, the trip let it out. Wherever they went in the desert gambling Mecca, the two women were greeted in grand style. Everyone seemed to know Bert and treated her like an old friend, waiting on her hand and foot. Gram recognized some of the figures they had met from the newspapers. One was former gangster turned hotel operator, Moe Dalitz. But one incident in particular completely blew Bert's cover.

The two women were just finishing up dinner before a floorshow. Their table was right up against the stage. Right before it began, a handsome, well-dressed man rushed up to Bert.

My biological grandmother, Beatrice, who finally blew the whistle on Bert. Cannes, France, 1966.

"Oh, Alberta," the contrite man begged, "I'm sorry. I'm so sorry. They didn't tell me you were in town. I promise it will never happen again. Please forgive me." The man kissed both of Bert's hands and both cheeks. Gram recognized the man immediately.

It was Frank Sinatra.

"Your grandmother got the buzz," Don said. "She began to realize that Alberta was a gangster."

Gram reported to her daughter that Bert had some kind of ties with organized crime. Mom confronted Bert and her new husband, who argued that Gram was crazy. With

Bert, Bill Miles and Tichi Wilkerson with Jack Valenti, the newly
appointed president of the Motion Picture Association of America.
According to Don Richardson, Bert and Valenti knew each other prior
to her transition to Hollywood. In what capacity is not known. Don,
however, was clear that Bert had many contacts on the West Coast that
she had formed during her Manhattan club days. Los Angeles, 1966.

The Miles-Richardson Family. Cindy Wilkerson, Bert, Reneé
Richardson, Don Richardson, Bill Miles, Tichi Wilkerson, and
me. John Landberg and Connie Roberts (foreground) were
family guests. Coconut Grove, New Years Eve, 1967.

that, both mother and son knew they were in trouble. They
began a campaign to convince Mom that Gram was clini-
cally insane and needed to be committed. Presumably to
ease tensions, our family took a trip to Europe but this time
Mom footed the bill. Whatever the reason, upon our return,
Mom and Bill curiously presented Bert with an accounting
of her meals and hotel stays and said she needed to pay up.
Offended, Bert immediately went on the defensive citing
that she had given the couple some very expensive presents.
Their relationship quickly unraveled.

Bert had been living with us in Bel-Air, and Mom had
had enough. She wanted her out. Likewise, Bill Miles was
anxious to get rid of his mother. Her New York City police
bust had not made the West Coast papers, but for him, it
was only a matter of time before her past caught up with
her again and destroyed his perfect marriage.

"He [Bill] wanted to get her the hell out of town," Don
recalled.

And so Bert was summarily shipped off to Florida.

9

BERT NEVER forgave her son for banishing her from Bel-Air. She relocated unhappily to Miami where Don said she posed as a retiree. But even in "retirement," Bert could not go let go of her past life which still tugged at her. In exile, she purportedly made arrangements for men.[5]

Bert in "retirement" in Miami with friends, 1968.

In 1969, Bert was diagnosed with cancer. Unable to look after herself, it was decided by Bill Miles and my mother that she should move back to our Bel-Air home. According to Don, Reneé, was not included in any decision pertaining to her mother at this point. Both Bert and her brother treated her badly. The two often ganged up on her.

"They didn't think Reneé had a brain at all," Don noted.

Reneé was often drunk and unhappy with Bert about something, Don said. She hated her mother for running her life. In the mid-1950s Reneé had just split up with her first husband. One night she was visiting her mother at The Executive Suite. Bert tried to cheer her daughter up by fixing her up with a customer. Reneé became furious. Her mother balled her out. "Well, what's the matter with that? Why are you so uppity?"

"She considered this to be the worst thing that ever happened to her," Don noted.

But taking Bert back into our home was not an act of compassion on either Bill's or my mom's part. Before Bert arrived at our home, Bill finally came clean to Mom about Bert's past and the existence of her millions locked up in numbered Swiss bank accounts. He explained that while he had carried the cash, it was Bert who always made the deposits—he never knew the actual account numbers. He stressed that it was imperative they find out what they were before she perished. Up until then, Mom had been clueless about Bert's secret life. It was only my grandma who harbored suspicions.

After Bill imparted the facts about Bert's secret fortune, Mom became very interested. Whether this was just pure greed on her part or an act of revenge is unclear. In the end, though, she was on board with the idea.

In a race against time, the couple installed a hidden microphone in Bert's room that was wired to an intercom in the master bedroom. They saw this was their last hope of catching the coveted bank account numbers before her death.

"They were hoping she would talk in her sleep or something," remembered Don. She never did.

When Bert discovered the listening device in her room, she told her son in no uncertain terms that he wouldn't be seeing a penny of her fortune. Once again, she packed her bags and moved back to Miami.

In retaliation for her son's betrayal, Bert did everything in her power to give her illegal fortune away before she died. According to Don, all the capital Bert possessed in US banks was doled out to friends.

"Anyone who came to the house got something," Don recalled. One of the biggest recipients, according to him, was actor Larry Storch who had wed one of Bert's girls. "Yeah, Larry Storch I remember got a nice check." But exactly how much is unknown. There were also the charities, most notably the televangelists. Indeed, while she lived with us, Bert, from her bed, had the TV on all day tuned to televangelists who continually and shameless pleaded for donations. Don believed Bert's donations to these individuals were a way of purging herself and atoning for her dark past.

Yet despite giving away all her money that resided in the US bank accounts, Bill Miles knew that there were still untold millions unaccounted for sitting in Swiss banks. He knew this because he had physically carried the cash. Within days of her passing, and armed with a copy of his mother's death certificate and passport, Bill, my mother, and myself flew to Geneva where we trudged to every bank Bert had done business with in the vain attempt to recover her vast fortune. But despite the documentation, they politely but firmly stated that without the numbers to the accounts, there could be no access. To this day, I can still remember the futile arguments that took place with the bankers at each establishment. In the end, I saw it as karmic justice. Bert had done her job well. Only the Swiss banks got her money in the end.

10

As Don wrapped up his saga, the pink skies of dawn peeked out over the horizon. I finally asked him why he was telling me all of this. He tilted the last of his red wine toward his lips. "I had a major heart attack recently," he said. "So, I guess I'm feeling mortality is upon me. I needed to tell you this because no one else will."

It was at that moment when I remembered my guitar story which I relayed to him, sparing no detail—Bill Miles discovering and confiscating the instrument, putting me on trial in the living room, then later surrendering it to me.

"That's the part I don't get," I said. "Why would he return it to me?"

Don was thoughtful for a moment. "Oh, yeah," he said. "I remember that. When Bill wouldn't give you the guitar back, Alberta threatened him. She said he wouldn't get a penny of her money if he didn't give you the guitar."

So that was it. Bert finally came through after all.

My head was spinning from the details of Don's tale. I needed time to process everything I thought I had understood about my grandmother. I'll be truthful in saying I wasn't convinced of his story. This new picture of the prostitute and madam just didn't jive with the woman I knew and loved. I would go on to interview Don three more times, once with a tape recorder running. Along with the newspaper article of Bert's bust and Don's chilling confession I captured on tape, which still sends shivers down my spine, I finally had to reconcile with the truth—that Bert was not who I thought she was.

Don also exacted a promise from me—that I would not publish anything about what he had told me until after his demise. A few years later, on January 10, 1996 at the age of seventy-seven, Don passed away at his home in Van Nuys California.

Driving home in the early dawn from Don's house through the empty streets, my mind was awash with my own memories of Bert, especially of that early evening in Monte Carlo where the two of us sat on the balcony of the Hôtel de Paris, the intensity of the blue sea below us and the shock of that question.

"Do you carry condoms?"

APPENDIX

TRANSCRIPT OF PHONE INTERVIEW WITH DON RICHARDSON, AUGUST 19, 1992

WW = W.R. Wilkerson III

DR = Don Richardson

WW: Alberta serviced the likes of—it was Bing Crosby and it was Frank Sinatra too?

DR: Yeah, the names that she threw around were Bing Crosby, Frank Sinatra, Sammy Davis, who she said was a great favorite of all the hookers. The hookers thought he was such a great bang, they practically do it for nothing. And Crosby used to hole up in a hotel in New York for like a week or two at a time and call Alberta for hookers and he'd stay drunk, but he'd like them to be around naked.

Ed Sullivan is an interesting case. Ed Sullivan used to call her—I'm just reporting what she told me. She said that he used to call her and she would send over a gorgeous girl who he would never go to bed with, but he would just watch her. She'd walk around the pad and he'd look at her.

And Frank Sinatra… this is a nice little bit. The hookers reported to Alberta that he used to bring along a little attaché case with dainty aprons. Lacy little aprons. Which he liked to have them put on when they were naked and then he'd pull the bow in the back. You like that?

WW: That's great. But describe to me what the place looked like. You said it was very suave, very, very luxurious.

DR: What, her place?

WW: Yeah.

DR: Well, she never had a whorehouse. She had a night-club. And it wasn't luxurious. It was on, I believe, 2nd Avenue. It was called The Executive Suite. And from the outside it just looked like a store that was out of business because all of the windows were painted solid. There were no names outside at all. And when you went through this painted, solid doorway, you came into what looked like an unfurnished bar. It had little bare tables and wire chairs and a little bar and several telephones for privacy and there was the most beautiful women you've ever saw in your life walking around.

WW: And so basically you could choose what you wanted and go where? Upstairs presumably?

DR: No, no they would leave. They would go to the Astor in those days. They would go to The Plaza. They went to very good places. They go to The Waldorf.

WW: But you couldn't choose, I mean you had to—

DR: Oh, yeah no they'd picked—What they did was they were hostesses. And Alberta was sort of the madam of the bar. She had nothing to do with the whorehouse. She was just like the lady in charge of the bar. And she'd table hop and chat with all her celebrity friends. And then when pairs would couple up, they would just leave. She'd just make a mental note of who was leaving so she'd get her cut. And she arranged none of the rest of it. That's how she stayed out of jail.

WW: She did what?

DR: She just offered the hookers…and got her piece.

WW: So that's how she stayed out of jail.

DR: That's how she stayed—She never ran an actual whorehouse. The time, the thing that's in that thing that you've got. The laminated article?

WW: Yeah, exactly.

DR: That thing was sent to me by a designer friend in New York who said you shoulda used it to blackmail her to get back your house. That thing was the result of a new police chief and every time there was a new police chief they would raid the girls. That's what the DA's doing now. That's what this Hollywood hooker is about. And it just happened that she had, she had sort of semi-retired and she'd arranged the party for the children of the Rockefellers. And there were several gorgeous broads and Alberta sitting in the outer room waiting in her mink. And two of the nephews or something of the Rockefeller family were in there with the dames. And, and the new police chief wasn't in on the take so he was making his stand.

WW: Amazing.

DR: That's how they did it. They used to—they'd arrest them and that would teach them a lesson and then from then on they were in on the cut.

WW: I gotcha. But—

DR: She paid for years and years and years.

WW: But she kept herself out of jail because she didn't actually own a premise by which the activity took place.

DR: No. Nor did she arrange it. They arranged it.

WW: Gotcha.

DR: And one time I went to pick her up to take her to dinner and she had a little apartment near Bloomingdales. And I rang the bell and she came to the door somewhat disheveled in her robe. And this was when she was in her fifties for Christ's sake. Out came a big bellied guy in a white shirt pulling up his pants and she introduced him as one of the heads of the US Steel Company.

WW: That she was servicing personally?

DR: She was blowing him in the—[LAUGHS]. And then I took her to dinner. We didn't discuss it of course. But the things that she did discuss. I told you the story about Papa Louie?

WW: No, go ahead, I forgot.

DR: Oh, Papa Louie, Papa Louie's a dilly. Papa Louie— she somehow—she was married originally to a guy named William Miles who was a silent picture producer. That's for real. Because there was a cameraman that worked for me for—Clark, who actually saved letters from those times. And once gave me a gift of a letter from William Miles to one of the other early big characters in silent pictures. So, there—the letterhead and all that you know. So, he was actually a real person. He was the father of Reneé and Bill.

WW: Yeah. He had syphilis though right?

DR: Right. He got syphilis, and she dumped him. And he ended up in potter's field. There was a big to-do about that and Reneé was very upset, and I was going to move his bones out here she was making so much goddamn noise about it. I thought it was stupid, but I would have done it. Anyway, after he croaked she was left with two young children. Somehow she met Papa Louie. She used to say that she met him on a ship going to Europe or something. Probably working her way over.

WW: Now his business was again?

DR: Papa Louise was the mafia judge. Papa Louie was the final word on whether you lived or died. Whether you got off or punished or whatever. He was the mafia judge.

WW: Gotcha.

DR: He lived up in Harlem in what looked on the outside like a tenement and when you went inside, as soon as you got through the entryway, you were into a whole transformed building that had been torn and gutted. And had been redone with elevators and guard rooms and holding places for guys that were in trouble. And his own apartment was an enormous duplex done in Chinese restaurant style. I'm telling you what she said. With plaster Buddhas and all that kind of shit. And she used to arrive with takeout Chinese food, which he loved. He was a madman for Chinese stuff. And she was his girlfriend. And she told me that one time they did a real naughty thing. He was, he was sitting at the table where he did his judging. And his henchmen were around him and some poor couplet was standing in the middle of the room and there was a cover over the table. And just for sheer sport of it, he had her underneath the table sucking his cock—

WW: Oh my god.

DR: While he decided the life or death of this poor quivering—[LAUGHS]. She considers that one of the great triumphs of her life.

WW: And she actually told you this?

DR: Well, she didn't say she was sucking his cock, but what the hell was she under the table for?

WW: Yeah. Now my next—

DR: She never used a dirty word the whole time I knew her. She always talked about clean girls.

WW: She used to give me lectures on sex all the time and it never made any sense. Here I am thirteen-years-old in Monte Carlo, Bill Miles and my mother have gone out for the evening. We're sitting on the veranda and we're finishing our dinner just the two of us and she launches into this litany about sexual activity and condoms, condoms, condoms. This was in 1965. My next question is, she must've made a ton of money. Where did all that money go? Switzerland?

DR: The money went to Switzerland.

WW: Like in some Zurich account?

DR: The money went in, you know, numbered accounts, unnamed accounts. And when...when she got sick, by that time she was very pissed off at your mother. As I told you before, Willie, she and Bill Miles worked up this whole thing to catch your mother. She financed it.

WW: Yeah, exactly. The whole courtship.

DR: The whole courtship. She financed the courtship. She bought him a wardrobe and all of that. So once he got set and was married to your mother, your grandmother started questioning what did he do. What did Bill do? What was his career? Who was he?

WW: That's true.

DR: And he made up all kinds of crazy stories. He dealt in Arabian horses. I mean, you know, he had endless stories. And at some point Alberta, to take the heat off, took your grandmother on a trip. I don't know exactly where they went, but they also went to Vegas I think. And your grandmother then began to realize that Alberta was a gangster. Because wherever the hell she went, big guys like the guy at the Sands and all those guys were kissing her ass. Which I had seen when I was with her in places like Vegas.

WW: Sure.

DR: So your grandmother came back and reported to your mother that Alberta was some kind of a madam or a hooker or something. She got the buzz. And your mother would not believe it. Your mother just could not believe that this was not a love match.

WW: [LAUGHS]

DR: Even though I had watched the whole thing happen. So, Bill then decided to start to instigate getting your mother to put her mother in the nuthouse. Did you know about that?

WW: You mean my mother's mother? My grandmother?

DR: Your mother's mother. He started to maneuver your mother into believing that your grandmother was insane. That she was accusing Alberta of being a hooker and of him being a pimp. And that obviously she was insane. So, there was a great deal of discussion at that point between your mother and Bill Miles, which he kept reporting to Alberta. About putting her in the nuthouse. Getting her the hell out of the way.

Then he ran into the obstacle that he couldn't bust the trust.

WW: Yeah, that I remember.

DR: And he tried every way. I mean, he tried up and down and sideways to break the trust, but he couldn't do it.

WW: Did he actually tell you that that was his agenda too?

DR: No, he never, he never told me any of these things. This all was like conversations between him and Alberta, frantic conversations. One night when we were on a wagon-lit going through Europe. I was in the next compartment with Reneé. And he was sharing the room with Alberta believe it or not.

WW: Oh my god.

DR: And they talked all through the night. And I was right up against the wall and it was the goddamndest thing to listen to them. And at that point they were carrying money to Switzerland.

WW: And so that's how—they actually muled all the money to Switzerland. What in money bags?

DR: They used to carry it in money bags, yeah.

WW: Did they ever solicit you to do this?

DR: Yes, they did. They asked me at one point before I knew that she was a hooker. At this point I didn't know that she was a hooker. I just married Reneé. All I knew was that she had a nightclub.

WW: [LAUGHS]

DR: I didn't know anything. I was just this dumb about— this is your mother. I mean, who would ever dream of such a thing? So they gave us the gift of a wedding present of the grand tour in Europe and when we got to the airports, I thought they were being very generous to take us on this lovely trip. Bill got me into the john and said, "Here put this on." And I said, "What the hell is it?" And he said, "It's a money belt." And I said, "I don't want to do that for Christ's sake." And he said, "Aw come on, I mean you know we do it all the time." And I said, "Hey, I'm working for the US Steel Company." I was directing *The United States Steel Hour*.

WW: [LAUGHS]

DR: "I can't get into this." "Everybody does it. Anybody who makes money. I mean Alberta makes money in her club because she doesn't pay taxes." And she didn't say she's a hooker. It's just that she's taking the profits abroad. And so, I, like an idiot, put on the fucking belt.

WW: Oh my god.

DR: And at one point during the flight, I went into the john to examine what the hell I was wearing, and I was carrying a quarter of a million dollars.

WW: Oh my god. So she must've made an absolute fortune.

DR: Oh yeah. It was big, big money.

Then, then when she got sick, she was very mad at your mother because she had gone on a trip with your mother and Bill and they had sent her a bill and they sent her an account with her meals and her hotel stuff and all of that and she was very pissed about that. Because she claimed she had given your mother expensive presents and all this. I knew nothing about that stuff. But anyway, she was very, very miffed.

Then she got sick. And when she got sick, she was unable to stay by herself in Florida, so somehow she wound up in your mother's house. The plan then was for your mother and Bill to find out the numbers of the accounts in Switzerland.

WW: While she was at the house?

DR: Yeah, that was the—that's why they took her in. They didn't take her in out of compassion.

WW: Oh, now that—

DR: I mean your mother was no doll either you understand.

WW: Oh, of course, I mean that makes sense because why would they uproot her—

DR: Yeah, they also—your mother didn't like her and this was a way of finding out her deathbed conversation about where's the money.

WW: But the irony of it is, is in the final analysis she wound up giving it away to everybody who came to the door.

DR: Yeah, she did. She gave it to Larry Storch. She gave it to all kinds of people.

WW: Yeah, all, all kinds of people.

DR: Incidentally, Larry Storch met his wife in that little joint.

WW: Really?

DR: Executive Suite. Yeah, she was a $50 hooker. She used to invite me to dinner at the houses of various stars in Hollywood in Bel-Air and places. And number one of them was Red Buttons who's married to—

WW: Alicia Buttons.

DR: A $50 dollar hooker.

WW: Alicia Buttons?

DR: Alicia Buttons was the hooker...one of Alberta's hookers.

WW: Oh my god. So she knew Alberta Miles.

DR: Oh yeah.

WW: Jeez.

DR: And Larry Storch's wife was one of her girls.

WW: You told me that Bill Miles was some kind of incessant social climber and he was terrified that people would find out about his mother.

DR: Oh yes. That's why he demanded that she retire. Now, the way that the whole thing got blown out of secrecy. When I met her, the first time I met her, Reneé brought me to this club and I sat at a table with Reneé and Alberta came over and she was very charming and very sweet. Oh, before that she had sent Bill to visit me in the Village. I had this beautiful sculptor's studio on Waverly Place. I didn't know Bill Miles from a hole in the wall. But she sent this mysterious Tyrone Power type person. At that time he was quite good looking. It's hard to believe now, but he was then quite a handsome guy.

And I don't know whether he had dyed hair or what, but he was very sleek with dark hair, you know, and… very interesting personality. Spoke several languages. And he came just a—Reneé arranged and appointment and we had a couple of drinks in my apartment. And obviously, he was finding out who I was. And he found out I was a completely reputable television director…making very good money. The US Steel Company was paying me upwards of $4,000 a week.

WW: Oh my god.

DR: Every time I did a show. And I do a lot of shows. So, apparently I got his approval. All he wanted to find out was whether I was making a living.

WW: [LAUGHS]

DR: And then I was invited to meet Alberta. And I came to the club with Reneé, and we sat down at a table, and I looked around. I saw various celebrity types that were familiar faces and these gorgeous girls. But I didn't get the buzz. I just thought it was like a night spot.

WW: Exactly.

DR: You know, private little drinking club. And then Alberta came over and she couldn't have been more delightful. She was an absolute doll. A little weird in the head with love and romance and astrology. I mean, she was, had a head full of shit like Shirley McLaine, you know very mysterious stuff about superstitions and good fortune and all that kind of stuff. And we had this little chat, and I thought she was adorable. I thought she was a Damon Runyon character, but it never occurred to me in a million years that she was a hooker, and then that was it. So we got married and we were married for several months and then one night…we were living in Forest Hills in what had been Reneé's previous marriage house. And she was paying rent to her ex-husband. And one night the phone rang at about two in the morning. I had to get up at six, so it was hardly inconvenient, and it was Alberta making her one call from jail. And it came as a total shock to me. We got in the car, and we went to bail her out. And when I got there, she was in the tank with those girls that are in the picture.

WW: My god.

DR: And they were all in their minks. And with them were all the street broads, the starving poor little whores looking at these aristocrats. Well, I paid her bail and she cried a little and then the lieutenant showed up. He had hurried from his home. He even put on his uniform to look impressive. I guess he expected pictures in newspapers or something. He apologized and kissed her cheeks and hugged her and said, "This will never happen Alberta. I'm sorry. The guy's a jerk." And you know, all of that. And he ushered her to the door. And we took her home.

WW: My god.

DR: That's where I found out she was a hooker.

WW: My god. The part where Bill Miles and—

DR: Oh, I gotta tell you one bit that comes to mind now. I mean, these stories are all buried in cobwebs I don't even think about.

Reneé hated her mother.

WW: Yeah, but Bill Miles hated his—her mother too?

DR: They both hated her.

WW: Yeah.

DR: Because she maneuvered their lives, and Bill Miles hated her particularly because she was in the way of him marrying wealthy women. I mean once they found out that she was a hooker, he was out of business with Sacony Oil and Rockefeller and the Kennedys and all the people he had his mind on. He was looking to get a rich broad. And Carmen didn't matter that much because she was kind of a slob and a model and you know, so it was not a big deal, but if you were going to marry the daughter of a Kennedy or somebody, which is what he was aiming for, then he would be in terrible trouble if Bert was active, so he kept insisting that she's got to blow it and retire. And she kept saying yes, yes she's going to retire. And Reneé told the story one night when she was drunk and unhappy with Alberta about something, because they treated her very badly. Bill and her mother used to hire—used to gang up on her. And give her a very bad time. She was kind of a weak idiot anyway. So this particular night she confessed what she considered the worst thing that ever happened to her with her family and that was that she was in The Executive Suite one night, visiting Alberta, and Alberta tried to set her up with a guy. With a john.

WW: Oh my god.

DR: And then Alberta balled her out and said, "Well, what's the matter with that? Why are you so uppity?" This is after she had split with her husband.

WW: Oh my god. Well, you know the argument that was in the train? In Switzerland?

DR: Yeah.

WW: Did that have anything to do with your honeymoon at that point?

DR: No.

WW: It didn't.

DR: No. They didn't even mention—they had no interest in us at all. They were just scheming and talking about the banks in Switzerland and future plans and all of that. They were like collaborating.

Alberta used to tell stories about how lucky the women were who had her son as a lover. She would tell endless stories about this dame wanted him and that dame wanted him. And he did…he did get around. I told you about the Barnum & Bailey lawyer.

WW: No.

DR: I didn't tell you about that?

WW: No.

DR: Oh, well the Barnum & Bailey lawyer when I used to go to New York to direct *The Defenders*, I used to stay in The Algonquin and one night Alberta came to The Algonquin and said, "You can't stay here, you're part of the family. I've got an apartment that I pay for for Bill." The one that your mother bought. "And there's no reason you can't stay there. Why do you have to pay these huge hotel bills?" So I said, "I like the privacy. I enjoy it." "No, no, you musn't…blah, blah,

blah." So I went there, and he charged me rent. I never told her, but it would cost me more than The Algonquin.

WW: [LAUGHS]

DR: Between the rent and him putting the touch on me every time he went out the door he'd say, "You got a fifty on you? I'll give it back tomorrow." I never saw a nickel. So he cost me double what it cost to stay at The Algonquin. And at The Algonquin I had a nice room, and at his place I had the backroom which was unfinished where they kept the maid shit.

And, wait there was a point to this.

WW: Well, you were going to tell me about some liaison he had with the Barnum & Bailey lawyer.

DR: Oh yeah. So one night—various nights he used to be invited to places, to society parties and things and I can remember stuff where like his studs were in hock and I pinned them together with paper clips. I actually pinned them up.

WW: How can he be in hock if there was this money around though?

DR: 'Cause he used to blow all of it.

WW: Oh, okay.

DR: She bought him a gas station, and he blew it. She bought him all kinds of shit. He also went to Europe and stayed for a couple of years and wrote checks forging her name. Could've put him in jail.

WW: What, they put him in jail?

DR: She could've.

WW: Oh, she could've put him in jail.

DR: She said, "You see how much I love him that I didn't put him in jail?"

WW: Oh my god.

DR: But any way, I pinned him up this particular night with the paper clips and he went off to this party and then about one in the morning he came back very excited. He had won a case of beer. Can you believe this?

WW: Oh my god.

DR: He didn't even drink beer. He had won a case of beer in some kind of a stupid prize. Some terrible picture of some goddamn thing and I had to come out in the hall and help him lug in the beer. That was the kind of stuff he'd go to. Where they had raffles or hunts for different things. I mean, you know, party games.

WW: Exactly.

DR: And one night we were waiting to go across the street. He had invited me to dinner at the home for the attorney the Barnum & Bailey circus. The chief attorney.

So, while we were waiting, I was sitting in the living room and he was in the bedroom getting dressed and there was a friend of his, who looked like an Italian. Another very handsome gigolo type. And the two of us were watching television. And in between they would chat a little bit through the door. Bill'd come out and tie his tie or something and they would talk about somebody's daughter. They were both into the same bit about rich women. And the show that was playing on television was Don Juan in Hell starring George C. Scott and this guy got interested in it and he was sitting looking at it and he said, "Hey that's a hell of a show." And I said, "Yeah it is." And then the credits came up and there was my name. And he said, "Isn't that—isn't that you?" I said, "Yeah." I said, "Bill never said you do that." So, Bill had never told anybody what I did. You understand that?

WW: Jeez. My god.

DR: Nothing. I was like some bum who was lucky to be married to his sister.

WW: My god.

DR: Anyway, then the guy left and we went across the street, Bill and I. And when we got to this great apartment—huge. It was the penthouse. Absolutely stunning. There was a very beautiful French woman who was in her thirties. And a daughter who was about fifteen, cute, cute daughter. And then the husband, the lawyer, who was a very dignified guy in his late fifties, I would say, early sixties and the action that

I saw was astounding. What I saw was that Bill came in, was kissed by the mother, kissed by the daughter, fondled by the mother. The daughter sat on his lap and wiggled a lot and blew in his ear. And the father of this group was making the greatest martinis I ever drank in my life.

WW: My god.

DR: Russian vodka. Made out of potatoes. Fantastic vodka. Anyway, we were chatting and he paid no attention to what was going on on the couch. They were practically getting screwed, the three of them.

WW: My god.

DR: Then we went into dinner and the servants served this gorgeous dinner and when we got back to the apartment, I said, "Jesus, what is that whole arrangement there? Are you fucking the daughter and the mother?" He said, "Yeah." I said, "Well the kid's only about fifteen. It's statutory rape." He said, "Oh no. They're not going to squeal." I said, "Well what's with the man?" He said, "He's got a bad back. He wears some kind of a corset, brace or something. He can't fuck his wife. So he tolerates our arrangement." He says, "As a matter of fact he gives me money."

WW: Oh my god. There was another incident that you told me too about some English photographer. Do you remember that story?

DR: Oh, yeah, yeah. The English photographer story was I would arrange in advance to have the apartment with the hope that I could move into the front room, that Bill would be on a trip somewhere, which he did frequently. This particular time I was promised the apartment on certain dates and when I got there, there were two people already in it. An English couple. A very wealthy English couple. And the guy showed me that afternoon he'd gone out and bought a whole big Hasselblad set with like two cameras and all the lenses and everything. I mean it was very expensive stuff. The wife was very pretty. The wife looked sort of like Vivian Leigh. Petite. Very dark. Very pretty. And she had her goddamn underwear hung up all through the apartment, which was very annoying. And I was, again, back in the maid's room. Bill came home and he said, "Jeez, I forgot entirely about them coming. I remember I promised you the apartment, but you know it's one of those things." And so, we sat down to have some drinks. And while we were having the drinks, he and the wife, Bill and the wife, disappeared into his bedroom and I was out there with the Englishman. And together we drank a whole fifth of scotch while I watched this maneuver to see if anybody was going to kill anybody or what was going to happen. It was obvious that Bill was in there fucking this guy's wife.

WW: [LAUGHS]

DR: And the guy wasn't doing anything about it.

WW: That is incredible. There was also a Fellini story too. There was some kind of—

DR: Yeah, there was a Fellini story. There was also his night table. When I did get to stay in the big bedroom with the cupids over the bed and all that. He had a night table full of Japanese sexual paraphernalia. Dildos, a two-way dildo and a blow-up snatch and you know, all the usual accoutrements. French ticklers and the *Kama Sutra* and the whole, the whole stuff.

The thing with Fellini was that when we were in Europe on that trip, the wedding trip, he said, "Would you like to meet Fellini?" I said, "Gee, hell yeah, I'd like to meet Fellini." I always thought he was full of shit, but I thought who knows?

WW: [LAUGHS]

DR: So, he drove us out, way out on the Appian Way in the dead of night, quite a distance outside of Rome, to a gorgeous house that was the house of Dino De Laurentiis and his wife, Silvana Mangano, and they had a pool in the back that was carved into the cliff side. Gorgeous, the whole thing was absolutely stunning. And at the party was the entire Italian film industry. And one by one as these people entered, and joined the feast, which was enormous, they all hugged and kissed Bill Miles, who seemed to be a very old friend of all of them. I was amazed. Then in walked Fellini and hugged and kissed Bill Miles. And then Messina, his wife, the lady in *La Strada* kissed and hugged Bill Miles. Then Bill brought Messina over to introduce her to me and we sat there chatting and she had terrible body odor. I remember it was horrible sitting there with her. And then they introduced me to Fellini and we got into chatting about his work and what I thought how great he was and all. He was fascinated with television and he wanted to talk about television. But they all, that night, were admirers of Bill Miles.

WW: That is amazing. Would you consider Alberta to be one of the great madams or was there somebody above her at that time?

DR: She was supposed to have been the biggest madam after—*A House Is Not a Home*. What the hell is her name? Shit, the lady, the lady who wrote *A House Is not a Home*. Incidentally, if you do a book, I have a picture nobody knows the source of except me that I can give you and it shows that lady, the original great—I'll think of it in a minute—Polly Adler.

WW: Polly Adler, that's right.

DR: She was the madam of the big gangsters. Mickey Cohen and all those guys. Al Capone. I have a picture of her when she graduated from night school in cap and gown.

WW: My god.

DR: That's a pretty funny picture.

WW: My god.

DR: You're welcome to it, if—

WW: Oh, I'd love it.

DR: If you don't say where you got it.

WW: Oh, no I won't say.

DR: It's a riot. She's there in her cap and gown with her little doggies posing for the picture.

WW: That's incredible. How did Bill Miles ever end up on your Alma Mater? Do you remember that?

DR: All I knew was that when I went out to teach at the academy in California, they asked me to come out there and be the dean and then I found out it was a real shithouse and I quit. But when I first was asked to go out there by the people in New York who were running the academy who were old friends of mine, and I was one of the last survivors of the original school.

WW: What was the school called again?

DR: The American Academy of Dramatic Arts.

WW: Yeah, okay.

DR: I went out there and at that point I was very interested in helping the school to succeed. At this point, the people ask me anything about it, I tell them it's lousy. In my book, I said it has no relation to the original. Anyway, one day the guy who was running it, who was originally a student of mine back in 1948 at the academy—his name was Toma, Michael Toma. He had very little background. I mean they were down to nothing. His only claim to fame was that he was the stage manager on several shows and he played a small running part on *Eight is Enough*. He played the coach. So he was a very inept guy to be running the American academy at all. That was one of the things I got as a sign that the thing was falling apart. And one day he told me with great pride that they had just added this multi-millionaire to their board of directors and I said, "Who is that?" and he said, "Bill Miles." And I got hysterical. And he said, "What are you laughing at?" And I said, "He's my brother-in-law and he's a pimp!"

WW: [LAUGHS]

DR: And this guy said, Toma said, "What are you talking about?" I said, "He is a pimp. He hasn't got a nickel. He just marries rich women." So I sent a wire to Bill Miles and I said I was split up with Reneé at that point and they were deviling me for money and I was giving them the house and all that. And he was giving me a terrible time on the telephone defending his sister. And in one of these calls right after this incident, I said to him, "I just saw your name as one of the people on the board of directors of the American academy and that's my alma mater and if you don't send your resignation in tomorrow, first thing tomorrow morning, I'm going to tell the whole story." So he resigned.

WW: [LAUGHS] So he was very careful always to keep that story under wraps.

DR: Oh yeah. Oh, oh yes. That thing that you've got. He would give you the chicken business.

WW: My god. Maybe I should go up and claim it.

DR: You can go have a free chicken whenever you want. You can own the ranch.

WW: Well, let me ask you something. You remember that ranch too, god.

DR: I never saw the ranch.

WW: Oh, okay. At some point, Alberta bought herself a seat on the New York Stock Exchange. Am I correct?

DR: I don't know about that.

WW: Okay, because at some juncture—see my sister told me after I came to see you last year, you know, when…I went to my sister and I said, "Did you know at all that Alberta was this and that." And she said, "Oh yeah, Alberta told me everything. And as a matter of fact she had a 'business' in Florida." So she continued those activities, but somewhere in between—and it was—but somewhere in between she became, oh well, if you could ever become extremely respectable but she had a seat on the New York Stock Exchange, she apparently did very well.

DR: Entirely possible.

WW: Yeah. Unless, of course, that that's something they fed my mother and the rest of the family.

DR: Also possible.

WW: Yeah. But so, this is the one secret that Bill Miles wanted—

DR: Oh, that was the bane of his existence. He felt that that was what was ruining his life. When he married your mother, that was the highest point of attainment for a gigolo that there was. And he then, he was part of the reason she moved to Florida. He wanted to get her the hell out of town.

WW: Now the interesting thing is that there was no question that he detested her, but she actually worshiped him. I mean—

WW: Worshiped. And worshiped him romantically.

DR: Oh my god.

WW: Do you think anything took place?

DR: Well, that night that we were in the wagon-lit I was itching to hear any sounds of kissing or cock sucking or—or anything. And I didn't hear anything.

WW: [LAUGHS]

DR: They talked all night.

WW: God almighty.

DR: But she was definitely romantically in love with him. She would talk about him as though he was the greatest cocksman that ever lived and all-around greatest catch for any woman. She didn't feel that she was imposing on these women at all. She was doing them a great favor. You know the first time I met your mother, all these talks that went on between Alberta and Bill and Reneé—Reneé was only sort of a bystander because they didn't think she had a brain at all. But a lot of the talk used to go on while I was hurrying through my dinner to go make my camera script or something. I was never party to their deals because I was separate. I was never part of their business, you know what I mean? I had my own business. So they paid no attention to me. I was just like somebody in the family who just sort of was around. And I remember all of the planning and the scheming when he first met your mother. I remember Alberta taking him down to Rodeo drive and all those places to buy the clothes, putting money in his account, arranging restaurants for him to take your mother to. Then finally came the night when I was to meet your mother. And on those occasions, they used to use the fact that I was a television director of some note as an advantage, I'm saying otherwise it meant nothing. So, I came to the restaurant with Reneé and there was—Alberta wasn't there. Bill was there with your mother. And your mother was the dearest, sweetest, nicest, gentlest, you would never have imagined her running *The Hollywood Reporter*...or being a tough dame. She was absolutely cow like, docile. Leaning on his shoulder and hugging him and totally in his possession. And I watched it abstractedly because I'd seen him do the same thing with so many other broads. It was like he had an opiate that he used to give them, you know. [LAUGHS]

WW: [LAUGHS] God that's amazing.

DR: Yeah, when you think of your mother in that situation, it's wild that she fell for him, but then obviously she always falls for him.

WW: But then, you never told her anything, I mean, during the marriage, I guess.

DR: Of course not. I didn't know her. I didn't know her at all. I had no—I had no connection with her.

WW: Jeez.

DR: The only way that I knew her. I don't think we ever had a conversation. The only way that I knew her was that she would invite me to a party at your house. And she'd be busy with all the other people. And like that, but I never... One night she and Bill came over with Alberta and I cooked them a big pot of spaghetti with some special sauce that would give you a heart attack. And they ate gallons of it. And even that night we all got drunk and nobody talked. I never had a conversation with your mother.

ENDNOTES

1 Don Richardson, interview, 1993.
2 Don Richardson, interview, August 19, 1992.
3 Ibid.
4 New York Journal-American, Friday, November 7, 1958.
5 Cynthia Wilkerson, interview, August, 1992.

ACKNOWLEDGEMENTS

I interviewed Don Richardson four times for this story and I'm grateful for every oppovrtunity. Equally, I'm grateful to Don's widow, Laura, who graciously loaned her husband to me to freely traipse through the distant past.

I'm also grateful to my sister, Cindy, for her remembrances and insight.

Thanks also to my editor and interior designer, Amie McCracken, who lovingly guided this text into safe harbor.

Finally, much thanks goes to my son for his encouragement. He gave me the courage to tell this story at long last.

ABOUT THE AUTHOR

Raised and educated in England, W.R. Wilkerson III graduated from the University of Southern California in 1977. He has authored several books including *Hollywood Godfather: The Life & Crimes of Billy Wilkerson*, *One Vote, One Person: How Changing Our Voting System Will Get Us Out of the Mess We're In*, and *The Man Who Invented Las Vegas*. He has contributed to several publications including *The Los Angeles Times*, *The Hollywood Reporter*, *USA Today*, and *The LA Weekly*.

wrwilkerson.net

INDEX